"May this book help you to connect to the Blessing of the Lord for your life, marriage, future, and destiny. And may the Lord give you a lasting testimony!"

This book is a gift from: ....

To: ....

Date: ....

Grown & ALONE

Dating With Purpose in Mind

MIKE DEAN

GROWN & ALONE

DATING WITH PURPOSE IN MIND

GROWN & ALONE: Dating With Purpose in Mind
Copyright © 2021 by MIKE DEAN

ISBN PAPERBACK: 978-1-7365259-1-3
ISBN HARDBACK: 978-1-7365259-2-0

Published by:
POWER CITY PUBLICATIONS
598 S. Harris Ave.
Columbus, Ohio 43204

All rights reserved under international copyright law. No part of this publication may be reproduced or transmitted in any form or by any means electronic or mechanical, including photocopying, recording, or any information storage and retrieval system, without permission in writing from the author and publisher.

All Scripture quotations are taken from the Authorised King James version and The New King James Version of The Holy Bible, except otherwise indicated.

For further information, please contact:

Pastor Mike Dean
POWER CITY CHURCH
598 S. Harris Ave.
Columbus, Ohio 43204
www.powercitychurch.org
6146537869

National Library of US Cataloguing in Publication Data
A catalogue record for this book is available from the United States National Library.

Editing and Design: **www.kingsviewbooks.com**

Printed in the United States of America

DEDICATION

I dedicate this book to everyone out there who earnestly wants to get the best out of the dating process by doing it right – dating with purpose and intent.

INTRODUCTION

" It's easier for a man to find a good woman than it is for a woman to find a good man..."

This book is geared towards assisting you with finding your "Why?" before you say, "I do."

But before we go too deep into all there is to say, I want to ask, "What matters to you in a relationship?"

You see, you need to clearly define what matters to you.

Excuse my ebonics but, what really matters to you?

Does race matter?
Does age matter?
Does education matter?
Does money matter?
Does intellectual capacity matter?
Does having a relationship with God or being a part of a religious group matter?
Does political affiliation matter?

What matters to you?

What do you want in a relationship?

Do you know what you are looking for?

Do you think you're going to get everything you want?

Is there a right way and a wrong way to date?

Why is dating so complicated?

Or, why is it so hard for you to date someone with similar goals in mind?

Well, this book is not all about problems, but much more about solutions. However, understanding the problem can help you make sound decisions when it comes to dating.

Okay, let's make a little switch: Have you ever thought to yourself, "Why am I not married?"

Or let's take a little step back, "Why am I alone?"

"Is it because...
- "I'm too demanding?
- "I'm not financially stable?
- "I'm not attractive enough?"

"Why did I get divorced?"
- "Was it finances?
- "Was it a lack of physical intimacy?
- "Was it a lack of spirituality?
- "Was it the lack of growth and personal development?"

Do you feel like you settled and it caught up to you?

Did you marry just because you had kids with each other?

Were you ever in love in the first place?

What happened?

Throughout this book, there'll be questions that come up from time to time. And don't be alarmed, those questions are to provoke you to think about where you are, where you're going, and how you're going to get there. It is not an indictment on you as a man or woman but perhaps, a guide, if you will.

Listen, we all have made and will continue to make mistakes along the way. But it is very important that when choosing a spouse, you do your due diligence in, at least, choosing the one that is as close as possible to your version of Mr. or Mrs. Right.

Life is too short to choose Mr. or Mrs. Wrong again.

The bottom line is simply this, you want to be happy. And you'd like to make your choice to achieve that.

I get it; I really do.

But can you explain and/or define your version of "happy?"

Oh, I hear you, Fred, "She has to be fine like the most expensive bottle of wine."

Oh… Suzzy, I can hear you too, "He has to be tall, dark, and handsome." I've heard that before…

Hey! Suzzy, how long do you think tall, dark, and handsome is going to last?

And Fred, how long do you think fine like aged wine is going to last?

Relationships are much more than what the outward appearance gives. Don't take this like I'm minimizing being attracted. And to be perfectly clear, an attraction is the magnet that brings two people together.

Let me say that again... "Attraction" is the magnet that initially brings two people together. YOU SHOULD BE ATTRACTED!

But it's important to note that some people aren't just attracted to how the person of interest looks. People are attracted to other things outside of how people look.

Now, let's play a game!

GAME TIME!!

Halle Berry has a great outward appearance but she has a Wicked Witch of the West attitude. Is that what you want? Yes/No

Brad Pitt has the most handsome looks but he

isn't there for his children. Is this what you want? Yes/No

Or, do you want someone who looks good on the outside, but can't stand people?

"Oh, but he says he loves me..."

Riddle me this battle man...

In my Riddler's voice, how much does the outward appearance go into what you're attracted to?

Hey! Fred and Suzzie, putting the outward appearance of a person aside, tell me, what else are you attracted to?

Come on, let's be grown for just a moment.

Attraction alone can't keep two people together.

Well, I need you to make up your mind!

Pause for a brief moment, and think:

Marriage can be fruitful, full of love and understanding, but it takes 'two' to make things go right. This is true! We know that many marriages end in divorce - religious and political affiliations notwithstanding. It's a real thing that happens daily.

I don't want to spend a bunch of time speculating on reasons why people end up in a divorce court. But might I suggest to you that people who end up in a divorce court just don't wake up one day and say, "I want to have a divorce."

No man, something happened that caused a wedge between the two.

How can you love someone one day and the next day completely hate them?

That doesn't make sense. Right?

So, there is an amalgamation of reasons why marriages end in divorce. Something happened that initiated a process, which eventually got to the point of no return. Perhaps, the couple couldn't figure a way to work it out.

Well, whatever the reasons are, every couple can always point to some things - a wedge between them, which they may have overlooked while in the relationship.

A breakup usually begins with one problem. From there, more problems begin to manifest and produce fruit after their kind. Thus, the problem takes root in the relationship, and soon produces the fruit of eventual departure from each other.

Can we go a little deeper?

Here's a good example!

Rob and Janet had an argument about Rob's ex-girlfriend/mother of his first child. Janet doesn't trust Rob around his ex, for the simple fact that Janet believes Rob still has feelings for his ex.

Rob tells Janet over and over that nothing is going on with him and his ex. Janet doesn't believe him...

Let's examine this closer...

What's the problem here? And what is the wedge between Rob and Janet?

Okay, I'll give you the answer this time... 'Trust.'

In Rob's mind, he's tired of being confronted by his wife every time he picks his son up for his court appointments. He can't deal with not being trusted by Janet, which breeds resentment in his heart, especially for her false accusations.

With each argument they have over this issue, Janet's mistrust feeds the wedge between her and Rob.

The sad part in all of this is that Janet may not even know how her mistrust of Rob is affecting him. Since she doesn't trust Rob, she does things that people who have trust issues do, leading to a lack of communication, intimacy, and more.

Why?

Well, who wants to be with someone who is constantly accusing them of things they aren't doing?

Now, Rob tells Janet, "I want a divorce."

She wonders why her distrust so seriously affects her husband who is trying to be a good father to his child.

What does this tell us about Janet?

That she has trust issues!

What we should be able to agree with, is that Janet wasn't born with trust issues. She probably had some unresolved trust issues before she said, "I do".

I'm sure you can see that dating a person who is wounded is dangerous...

You don't need to be in a hurry.

There's no need to demand things you aren't ready for.

This is why dating with purpose is important!

I believe the problem for many singles is this: You've been dating without purpose. You've been dating without the primary goal to, one day, move to a higher form of a relationship, which is marriage.

Once you understand and apply some simplistic principles, I believe you will see dating from a different perspective.

When you date without marriage in mind, you cheat your destiny. Time, money, and energy are wasted on someone who does not share the same interest.

Now, imagine how many Robs and Janets are out there who enter relationships that could have been long-lasting, with rather unresolved issues that end up destroying their union.

Yes, love is very, very important! But unresolved issues like distrust, disrespect, and many more, flat-out destroy relationships like a meteor hitting a vulnerable planet.

This book is a road map to having a long-lasting marriage. But there is a lot of work to do in the meantime for that to take place.

Now, for all of my Biblical scholars, there is not much within the Bible when it comes to dating.
The Bible talks a lot about parenting, through principles and stories. And the Bible probably talks more about marriage when it comes to relationships, more than anything.

There are reasons for that and I'll share just a few...

You must note that much of the Old Testament was written about the Children of Israel, from the creation of Adam to the flood, to the promise made to Abraham.

God established His chosen people through Abraham's seed. And with that in mind, many laws and practices came to play in those times.

Marriages were arranged. Think about it... God arranged Adam and Eve's marriage. Abraham instructed his servant to arrange the marriage of Isaac.

Please, don't get me started on this four-letter word we all want in a relationship... Love... Yes, we all want it.

Now, there were other cases in the Bible where the marriages weren't arranged. However, it still says nothing about the process they went through before they got married.

What I can safely say is that this book is not about dating just so you can show a beautiful lady off to your friends, or prove your mother wrong; nor will this book placate your ego.

This book is meant to give you an enabling seed for a fruitful marriage when the time is right. It will properly guide you in your journey towards a long-lasting marriage. And, I know you'll be back to share your testimonies!

Shalom!

PREFACE

As human beings, we are designed with an innate list of needs and desires that we tend to follow without much thought.

Maslow's Hierarchy of needs has become one of psychology's greatest ways to pinpoint our needs and shows the importance of each need to our day-to-day lives. The bottom of the pyramid is our psychological needs, that's, the things we must have, to survive at the simplest level on earth.

We all need food and water, air and sleep, clothing, and somewhere to protect us from the weather. As we find things that give us our simplest needs, we allow ourselves to look for more abstract needs, or those we can't simply go to the store and pick on the way home. Once our body has been taken care of, we start looking for ways to ensure we will be safe. We look for personal security, a job to make sure we'll have resources to take care of our psychological needs.

Most of our childhood and adolescence is spent learning how and where to acquire the things we need for the first two sections on the hierarchy of needs. We spend most of our childhood learning what is expected of us to know when we head off to college, how to keep a job, even if it's simply a cashier at McDonald's.

We're taught what to look for when it's time to get a place of our own, and how much we should expect to spend when shopping for groceries. Throughout our entire lives, we have classes that give us the in's and out's of adulthood when it's our time to make sure we're taking care of those needs. But as we reach higher in the pyramid of needs, the available lessons on how to accomplish those needs start to wither.

It could be my upbringing or the school I went to, but I know I've never been to school and sat in a class where they taught us about love and belonging. Love, even though it's merely four letters, is one of the most complicated and searched-for parts of being human. And we all experience it. We all know the pool in our hearts that demands to be shared and poured into.

The beginning of art on this planet began with our first attempts to describe love. But most of us never had a lesson on love and belonging. Most of our knowledge on intimacy and a sense of connection came from where we spent most of our time. The things we absorbed, being around those we're quite sure we do love.

Our desire for intimacy, as mentioned before, is an innate feeling we have. As long as the heart beats, it will make its desire "to fill and be filled" known. Even the hardest and harshest of mankind has something they allow to break down the barriers to their innermost self.

Thankfully, not all types of love are as complicated to accept. We readily accept the love from our parents and siblings. Even though there may be times when we don't like our family members, the DNA we share invokes the need to make sure they are happy, and our desire to share our happiness with them.

As we grow and meet new people, we start

friendships. Bonds are made by choice but bonds matter to us nonetheless. We look for our friends through our times of need. We spend time with them because the flexibility of friendship isn't always seen in our ties with our family. We all have stories of things we've done with our friends that we would never let our siblings tag along with. And those bonds make sense.

These types of love are the foundation of who we become as a person. And speaking so plainly, it almost doesn't make sense why I stated love was complicated; it's easy to agree with that sense of intimacy and love with our family and friends. But we all know that if the word "love" or "relationship" is brought up in a conversation of hypotheticals, baking cookies with mama or playing video games with our siblings may not be the first image that pops up in our head.

If we're walking down the sidewalk and overhear someone tell their friend, "But I love him," we're not going to assume they are talking about their childhood pet. No, we think of romantic love: that love that causes wars and breaks people down; that love that we've spent millennia trying to understand and illustrate from everything - poetry, music, paintings, and dance.

Even if we don't truly understand love, we all know what it feels like to start that crusade of acquiring love to fail. Every great musician in history has at least one song where he or she has wailed into the abyss, talking about the pain of lost love. The cons of failing to acquire this love are so great and so well understood that many of us would rather lock ourselves in our rooms than admit to anyone but ourselves that we want romantic love.

But that's okay.

It's understandable.

And as long as we acknowledge the fear of love, we can move past it. But first, I must ask the question, what makes romantic love that much harder to obtain and maintain?

One of the biggest differences between romantic love and other types of love is how it begins. With our friends and family, our proximity to them is what starts the relationship. The intimacy between us and our family and friends starts simply because we see them all the time.

We're there in their corners for their accomplishments and failures because... well, we were in the other room when they decided to try it out. And while proximity (almost by force sometimes) is the beginning of our relationships with our friends and family, it's a goal when searching for a romantic partner. It isn't something that we readily give someone. Even if we decide to start a romantic relationship with one of our friends, the dynamic of the relationship is expected to change so drastically that all of us have decided to forego that option for fear of losing the relationship we already have.

In our relationships with our family and friends, there's almost a mutual understanding that these relationships are only allowed a limited amount of the several facets that make up who we are as a person.

We're allowed to keep certain doors closed; and even expected to, as we grow older. It might not be that way when we're younger. But as we grow, we get accustomed to the idea that certain doors open with the key of a particular relationship, and there are doors where that key doesn't work.

As we go through life, there may be doors that certain relationships aren't even allowed to see, let alone know they can't open. But that isn't the case in a romantic relationship. In those relationships, we are expected to give all of us, with all our doors and keys, in exchange for all of them and all their doors.

And so we begin the gruesome and tiresome process of dating. We mark down what we want from a partner and we go on a conquest to find them, proving to them they will want us in their lives as much as we want them in ours. But there's a reason, "It's a good plan until you bring people into it" is the quote. We get it wrong more times than we get it right, and with each time we get it wrong, we add another door and wall to our inner selves.

With that, welcome to "Grown and Alone," where we will talk about how to appreciate and obtain that type of love we have tried so hard to grab in our hands. Though obtaining romantic love feels more at times like we're trying to strangle water, we will speak on how to figure what we really need and desire, and the things we are willing to accept and those we are not.

Our first destination on this 'Journey to dating' is Dating with Intent, where we'll attempt to lessen the time we spend looking for Mr. or Mrs. Wrong.

Table of Contents

Chapter 1	Dating With Intent	1
Chapter 2	Enough About Me...	9
Chapter 3	Resumes and...	23
Chapter 4	Credit and Other Things	39
Chapter 5	Meeting the Family	56
Chapter 6	(S)he Got Kids	67
Chapter 7	S.E.X	76
Chapter 8	Love Languages	85
Chapter 9	The Near and The Far	92
Chapter 10	Keeping God First...	101
Chapter 11	If it isn't Love	108
Chapter 12	That's all Folks	114

1

DATING WITH INTENT

> **"DATING CAN BE ONE OF THE BIGGEST OBSTACLES YOU FACE IN LIFE, BUT THE OBSTACLE COURSE FOR ROMANTIC LOVE CAN BE HARDER IF YOU LACK PURPOSE AND INTENT."**

Have you ever tried to learn a new skill? Maybe it was learning a new language or a musical instrument. It could have been learning how to throw a faster fastball, or how to play chess so you could finally beat your grandfather fair and square.

Almost all of us remember trying to learn how to ride a bike. Do you remember how you felt the first time you tried… only to fall with a bike on top of you? I pray my readers were allowed to fall in the grass, but many of us remember picking gravel out our knees when we fell.

Whoever was teaching us would have told us to get up and try again. But it wasn't their words that got us back on the bike. No matter how many times someone could tell us, "This time it will be different, just get back on." That's not what kept us grabbing on to the handlebars.

They could have said those words until they were blue in the face and it still wouldn't have mattered. It wasn't their direction or words that got you back on the bike, but your intent. If you didn't really want to learn how to ride a bike, you would have walked away from the bike, declaring it wasn't that important to you. You could have thrown that helmet on the ground and decided to go play outside in another way, maybe deciding a scooter was the right way to go. But if there was a purpose to you falling; if you had your mind made up to get back up, then you would.

So what is the difference between purpose and intent? Well, your purpose of being there was to learn how to ride a bike. But your intent wasn't to learn. Your intent was simply to ride a bike.

Dating can be one of the biggest obstacles we face in our lives, I admit. But the obstacle course for romantic love can be harder if we lack purpose and intent. Imagine trying to complete hurdles on the track field with ten-pound ankle weights on. Purpose and intent allow us to take the ankle weights on, allowing the track to be easier, but also makes it harder for us to stray and settle for things that do not align with our intent.

There's no judgment passed toward anyone who strays, we've all done it before. We've all settled for something that looked sweet when we first saw it, only to see the rotten core after it was much too late. I don't have the power to tell you your final goal. That's something you must acquire. I aim to nudge you in the right direction. And so I ask, what conceives your choice to date (again)?

We all get this ache in our hearts, the persistent one that waits until you have no distractions for it to rear its ugly head. For most of us, we begin *the dating life* again to relieve the ache of loneliness in our lives and replace it with connection and intimacy. We may see many of our childhood friends tying the knot. Our homeboys who went to the club with us now spend their time watching Netflix with the love of their lives. Or maybe you're just tired of being the bridesmaid and never the bride. This little worm in our head uses all types of thoughts as its food.

It continues until one day we look up from our autopilot and believe we have something missing.

We all share that moment where we feel there is a place in our heart that's lacking nourishment. And like all emotional aches, this ache rarely pops up when we're out enjoying ourselves. It typically pops when we're alone; even more so when we're surrounded by others but we still feel like the loneliest person in the room. Nothing nudges the desire to date quite like being the third wheel.

The main reason we start dating is to have someone to share our lives with, in all aspects of our lives. The person we want to see when we wake and when we go to sleep. As adults, we all understand that dating is an important path to finding that someone. And we all are, at least, somewhat knowledgeable about what it means to date someone.

But there's a difference between simply dating and dating with intent. What constitutes that difference?

To date with intent, you have to be aware and fully acknowledge the reason you entered the dating life, yes, but you also have to acknowledge the full you that you're bringing into the dating world.

Most would call dating with intent "serious dating" versus "casual" dating. Casual dating is usually seen as dating someone for a few weeks, or going on dates simply to pass time. Or because you need a date for someone's wedding and it's just too awkward to bring your ex along. Many would find it hard to describe any relationship that crosses the span of a few months as casual, as too much knowledge and time is spent within that period.

No matter the various forms we find ourselves in when it comes to casual dating, it can be summed up into one motive. Or better, one lack of motive. *Casual dating is any type of dating where the goal isn't to be with this person for the rest of our lives.* Any dating where we cannot see a future with our significant other shouldn't be seen as serious dating. In these pages, we will hit on casual dating seldomly. The intent of casual dating holds the same reason we picked up a T.V show that our friends told us about: because we're bored mostly. Most casual dating is desired as a distraction from our lives rather than something to add to it.

Dating with intent, however, is dating with the hopes of adding to our lives. In dating with intent, you are not only looking for someone who will be there in your present, but someone you can see a realistic and happy future with. We are looking for our person; the one who looks for you when they enter a room but also shares the ups and downs of life with you. I can't tell you what your reason for dating should be, but before we start the next chapter, ask yourself, *Why do I really want to enter the dating life again?*

THINK ON THIS!

1. If there was a purpose to you falling; if you had your mind made up to get back up, then you would.

2. Dating can be one of the biggest obstacles you face in life, but the obstacle course for romantic love can be harder if you lack purpose and intent.

3. Casual dating is any type of dating where the goal isn't to be with that person for the rest of your life.

4. When you date with intent, you are not only looking for someone who will be there in your present, but someone you can see a realistic and happy future with. If it were as easy to throw away your money as it is with your time, people would think you are not in the right mind.

2

ENOUGH ABOUT ME, LET'S TALK ABOUT YOU

> **BREAKUPS HAPPEN, BUT THEY AREN'T A DECLARATION THAT THERE WAS SOMETHING WRONG WITH YOU OR THE OTHER PERSON, BUT THAT THE RELATIONSHIP WASN'T MEANT TO BE."**

Funny enough, the most crucial and first step to dating has nothing to do with other people, but everything to do with you. The first step to dating has to do with you and your past, because the first step you have to take is taking the time to heal. Healing is very critical because it provides you with an opportunity to regain perspective and focus to remember what it meant to be in a relationship and not just what you allowed yourself to settle for.

Too many times, people think the cure for a breakup is to phase right into a new relationship.

Doing so doesn't give you the time to reflect and accept what your heart is trying to tell you. Most of the time, we search for rebound relationships (or flings) simply as a bandage for the pain we won't acknowledge. And while it is understandable, that doesn't make it okay. A lack of acknowledgment of our own hurt will cause us to bleed on anyone who tries to take that coveted position.

That's why in order to truly allow yourself to walk into the greatest future you can have, you have to take the time to acknowledge your past. This is true in all aspects of our lives, and relationships are no exception.

Now, we're not here to dwell in our past, but to deal with it. This chapter isn't for us to wallow, but to figure what went wrong and what went right so we can look forward and move toward a better future.

We all know the term "baggage" when it comes to dating. All the messy stuff that a person has when they come into a relationship that never seems to air out until one or both partners are mad at one another. But what makes something baggage? How is baggage any different from any other aspect of our pasts? Is mama being mad because my lady doesn't fix my plate at Thanksgiving considered baggage?

Baggage isn't something you offer in a relationship. Baggage isn't something you know you have and something you acknowledge. There's a reason the word "baggage" has such a negative connotation. Baggage is something unresolved, something from our past relationships we feel was never completed. Most of the time, our baggage is something we think of first when we think of dating again. We think about how not to add to this baggage but also, how to hide the baggage from our prospect in the dating life.

But I'm not here to teach you how to hide your baggage. I'm here to help you deal with it. And what's the hardest and easiest way to get rid of your baggage? You gotta stop rummaging through it. You have to put down the controller.

I don't know if you ever bought a video game that you just loved with all your heart; the type you'd spend countless hours on perfecting your playing style. You know how all the enemies work, and you could even give a Ted Talk on why one weapon works better than all the rest. Anyone who would call themselves a gamer (I'm just traveling down memory lane as a kid playing Nintendo) can think of a few games that could fall into this category. For anyone who has routinely played a video game, we all share the great feeling of doing something we enjoy. And we all remember that feeling of when life made us put the controller down.

Maybe we started college, or we got a new job. Whatever was the catalyst, somewhere in our lives we had to put down the controller to take care of responsibilities. And you know what happens when you put down the controller for too long? When you've gone months and months without playing that game? It no longer has the hold that it once did. You're not so willing to be up all night playing this game, and even when you have time to do so, the controls don't feel the way they used to. And after a certain point we get so tired of trying to re-familiarize ourselves with something that isn't so important anymore, we give up trying to play it.

When you first set the controller down, it feels like you're betraying yourself. You might get mad at your new classes or responsibilities because it takes away time from your game.

Our baggage is like a video game, something we like to play around in our heads and hearts without worrying about the consequences it might have in our current lives. We look forward to picking up the controller and playing the game.

We like thinking back on the good times, the moments that made our heart flutter. Even if we know we shouldn't, we pick up the controller to feel something besides the loneliness we feel. And most of us understand that we have to put it down, though it's hard to just walk away. But each time we put the controller down, it makes it harder to pick it back up.

Even harder still, is giving the controller to someone else. We've all had a Madea in our lives to tell us to "give it to God" when we're going through something. And I will admit, sometimes it's easy to give something away. It's easy to give it to God when it's something we don't want to think about, like our bills and our fears. It's easy to trust in Him to take care of the things we don't want. It's a little bit harder when it comes to the things in life we enjoy. You have to give God the controller when it comes to love. We've all been hesitant. When it comes to love, sometimes we can be like kids gripping tight on our favorite teddy bear.

In matters of the heart, it's almost second nature to doubt that God really has our best interests in mind. The hubris of the heart allows us to believe we are smarter when it comes to our desires and needs of romantic love. And so we constantly pick the controller back up, thinking that maybe if we try that level again we can beat it. Maybe if we put in a certain cheat code, we can win the game. But you gotta put that controller down. How can God pick up something that you're holding onto with white knuckles?

What stops us from putting down the controllers in our real lives? What forces us to pick up that baggage each time we wish to start anew with someone who had nothing to do with the last level we played? Our past, whether we want it to be or not, plays one of the biggest roles in what we believe we deserve in the future. Most of the time we don't put the controller down because we feel that that video game is the best we deserve. We feel whatever we had was the epitome of what we can offer. We drag down ourselves with the chains of baggage, making it harder to jump over hurdles to grab the best life we can. Unlike the video game where the love and concern we have for it can be washed away simply by ignoring it long enough, we have to acknowledge and deal with the games we've played in our lives.

Have You Seen....?

Acknowledging and dealing are easier said than done. I would never insult your intelligence by giving you a time span to deal with all the things you're afraid to deal with; my goal is to merely put you in the right direction. So, how do you acknowledge what went wrong and what didn't? You have to reintroduce yourself to the one person you'll be with all of your life: you. In most instances, the reason behind a failing relationship is that you forgot yourself. When I'm saying this, I'm not saying you forgot your name or where you come from, but you forgot who you were at the core. We've all done it to a certain extent before.

Relationships make it extremely easy to assimilate who you are into and what you think your partner wants you to be. But the lack of a relationship with a romantic partner makes it manifold easier to work on the relationship you have with yourself. Take advantage of solitude, it is not a punishment, but something we all need in our lives. Be like an NFL coach and go watch films to locate areas you need to improve on.

I'm not sure if you watch sports, but we all know the amount of effort and pressure athletes go through to play the best game that they can play. We're all aware that they work out, they eat right, and we all know they do these things on a level that we normal people (those of us who don't see the couch as a bad place to be) don't really have the time nor desire to do. We all know this part of the preparation for the big game. One of the lesser talked about practices these teams do has nothing to do with working out or eating, but watching a film.

No, I am not saying watching How Stella Got Her Groove Back is going to help you understand the dating world again, but this is a book. We'll resume our lessons once the credits roll...

*** *** ****** *** ****** *** ****** *** ****** *** ***

You back? Great. What I meant by watching the film in terms of sports teams is watching the film of their last performance. But the players aren't watching their last game in the same manner the fans were watching it when they played. They're not watching it for the entertainment part of the game, but as a critique. The fact that they can watch how they performed in prior games gives them a reference to what they need to work on, and what just needs a little polishing for the time being.

To step it a little further, they might even watch a film on the team they're about to play, so they can see what's compatible to get the prize they want. One thing is for sure, no matter what team is watching and preparing for the next game, they don't go to watch the film thinking there's nothing to improve on. They don't watch it just to show they're the best, but to get better. So, as you watch your own film, I would advise you not to go in because you want to see a highlight reel of what makes you God's gift to earth, but what can be improved on.

Dating in itself comes with a list of challenges and hurdles we all have to go through. The last thing you want to do for yourself is to go into the dating life blindfolded. No matter what our goals may be when we enter the dating world, we all have to understand we are not going to be the same person every time we decide to break the surface. And so, once you see your prize, you watch the film in order to prepare yourself.

There is a reason why people call love a battlefield, and it would do you no favors not to have your armor ready.

We will all have a specialized list of what we look for in our own films. Here are just a few things we all should think about when we're watching:

What impact did this relationship have on your relationship with God?

What impact did the relationship have on you?

What impact did the relationship have on your

family?

What impact did it have on your emotions?

What impact did this relationship have on your children?

What impact did this relationship have on your finances?

The thing I love most about the film room is the fact that it's not just the head coach watching the film, but the entire team; not just the players, but the defensive coach, the offensive coach, the special teams, and even the water boy, if he wanted to. The film room is as much a team effort as the actual game. And once you've taken your rightful position as head coach and you watch the film, you make the effort to figure out what's best for you. You confide and find counsel in your friends and family. Through meditation, prayer, and fasting you release the things that no longer serve you as you are. I say this because this part of getting ready for dating must be met with the intention of bettering yourself past dating.

The people in your life help assist you in evaluating who you were and who you are. Most of the time, this happens organically. One day you're spending time with your peeps and they notice the change in you. They notice the habits you've given up. Your family may take notice you don't move the way you used to, or you look happier now. Or, if you want to place your friends and family in a room and have an intervention about why your past relationships didn't work, you can. I wouldn't advise it because there might be some colorful words thrown out if they had something planned on the same night you wanted to come to Jesus' meeting.

I know I've mentioned it before, but I want to reiterate. You watch the film to understand what didn't work and what did. But you're not evaluating for the lone sense of getting ready for the next relationship. You shouldn't stop critiquing yourself the moment someone attractive walks by and you think it's time to dive in again. This should be a time spent getting back to your core self, understanding the needs and desires of your heart. This film-watching should be spent investing in your relationship with God and yourself, as they are the only two beings in this plane that you will be with every day of your life.

And understand that breakups happen. And not all breakups mean that something was wrong with either of the people in the relationship, but that the relationship wasn't meant to be. Now, there are some breakups that show yes, that compatibility was doomed from the start. But breakups aren't a declaration that there was something wrong with you. Remember this as you watch your film. All things come to an end, but there is hope in new beginnings.

All in all, the first step into dating again must be looking into ourselves to figure where we should go from here. Our first step to dating life shouldn't be seen as a way to make sure we're ready to date someone, but rather, where we want to be. Are we ready to add another facet to the many things that make us into who we are? We must be able to put down that controller and believe God has something better in store for us. Thankfully for us, letting go gets easier each time we try it.

THINK ON THIS!

1. Our past, whether we want it to be or not, plays one of the biggest roles in what we believe we deserve in the future. To truly allow yourself to walk into the greatest future you can have, you have to take the time to acknowledge your past.

2. You have to give God the controller when it comes to love. How can God pick up something that you're holding onto with white knuckles?

3. We drag down ourselves with the chains of baggage, making it harder to jump over hurdles to grab the best life we can.

4. You have to reintroduce yourself to the one person you'll be with all of your life: You. In most instances, the reason behind a failing relationship is that you forgot yourself.

5. The lack of a relationship with a romantic partner makes it manifold easier to work on the relationship you have with yourself. Take advantage of solitude, it is not a punishment, but something we all need in our lives.

6. There is a reason why people call love a battlefield, and it would do you no favors not to have your armor ready.

7. Through meditation, prayer, and fasting you release the things that no longer serve you as you are.

8. You shouldn't stop critiquing yourself the moment someone attractive walks by and you think it's time to dive in again.

9. Breakups happen, but they aren't a declaration that there was something wrong with you or the other person, but that the relationship wasn't meant to be.

10. All things come to an end, but there is hope in new beginnings. Letting go gets easier each time you try it.

3

RESUMES AND... "WHERE ARE YOU?"

>
> **A MARRIAGE SHOULD BE MUCH MORE THAN JUST BASIC DESIRES. YOU NEED SOMEONE WHO IS GOING TO BE BENEFICIAL, AND NOT JUST THE ONE THAT LOOKS GOOD FOR THE STOMACH OR EYES OR MAKES YOU FEEL GOOD."

In the first few steps of getting into the dating world, we create the ultimate resume for our applicants. How could we not, we've spent years building the ultimate spouse. They may look like a model or could make a lot of money. They could be a great listener, or maybe a good communicator.

Sometimes, we build our resume and knock out anyone who doesn't hit every check in it. They may be a great listener, but it's easy to see they haven't spent time in the gym for some time.

They may look like Aphrodite reincarnated, but the minimum amount of languages your dream girl has to speak fluently is three on a rainy day.

In this chapter, we'll talk about the difference between the resume we fantasize about and the resume that will be beneficial to our lives.

At first, the resume may be the simplest version anyone can find. The biggest expectation in the relationship may be a list of things you expect them not to do. And only the minimum of basic decency: Don't lie. Don't cheat. The list is full of all the things one should expect when they enter a relationship.

You just want your boyfriend to listen to you when you'd like to talk, and not just when it's obviously convenient for him.

You may just have a girlfriend who understands you have your projects, and your desire to be alone has nothing to say about your love for her.

But as we continue to risk our hearts to the quest for real love, our resumes change. The expectations are no longer things we should expect from a relationship, but more tripwires to our heart.

It may sound weird to throw a tripwire into a metaphor about the heart. Our hearts are the most precious things about being human, and we don't want to give that treasure over to just anyone. We would much rather test the waters to make sure the person we want to be in our lives is a good fit.

That's how we grow up thinking about love.

We're compelled to give off little pieces of love to anyone who may need it. Anyone could come into our heart, but after enough pain, we place tripwires over the entrance to our love.

Or, when our expectations were unmet or unfulfilled, what was once a revolving door becomes a room full of traps. And though we may not know how many traps we have across our hearts, we all know the feeling of insecurity when a tripwire goes off.

We need someone who will answer the phone immediately because if they can't answer their phone, it must mean they're doing something they don't want us to know about.

We need someone who is willing to cut off friends of the opposite sex because we're sure they want to have sex with our spouse.

The thing about tripwires? No one puts one down unless they expect someone to walk over it. No one puts tripwires around their heart unless they expect someone to hurt them. And we get hurt. Over time, the resume that only required the bare minimum of decency to our lives digresses towards a resume for someone who will not intentionally try to hurt us. Who knows that we will do anything for love and we expect the same for them, even if it means hurting ourselves?

Many problems that arise in looking for someone are rooted in defining the role you're looking for. Some may wonder what I mean by that, given that the role is obviously that of a husband or wife. That's the goal, right? I once agreed with that, but a husband or wife, when it comes to their place in your life, is their title.

We've all held jobs, and we know our job title doesn't define everything that comes into what our role in our company is. The General Manager of a McDonald's will have a different set of responsibilities than the General Manager of an Apple store.

Being your husband or wife is the job they were

interviewed for, but it wasn't the role on the resume. For many of us, the role of the applicant is someone who completes us. We've all known the feeling of speaking of a love where they become one.

Go to church and start a discussion about marriage and I can bet someone's going to quote the well-known passage of Genesis 2:24, (NASB): "For this reason a man shall leave his father and his mother, and be joined to his wife; and they shall become one flesh."

It is important to understand the one we speak of in this text, though I'm sure some of us have heard this verse when our parents have decided it's time for us to leave the nest.

There's an issue we rarely acknowledge when we incorporate the "one flesh" in that verse. It should be seen as one union, but at times, we may read those two words with the comprehension that we are incomplete; that as a single person, we are not whole.

And what do we do when we feel like we are incomplete? We look for someone who has traits we feel we lack in ourselves. Instead of looking to be one in a relationship, we start looking for someone who can make us a full human by proxy.

As long as we have the traits they lack and vice versa, we assume we've become one functioning person as long as we have each other. This sense of being incomplete conceives codependency, as we don't know what to do if we don't have the piece that makes us feel whole.

The reason we take the time to acknowledge ourselves, our past, and our desires before we enter the dating life is so we can easier accept the fact that we are indeed whole.

Since we are made in God's image, do you think He left pieces of you as a DLC? We have to deal so that when we are faced with an "I need someone to complete me," we can acknowledge that piece, and remember we are complete and whole within ourselves.

Another role that causes a problem is, "everything I ever wanted." Not every example of this role calls for our spouse to compensate for our lack, but rather, to give in to our desires.

We can be looking for someone who doesn't need Instagram to be a model. Someone who blows our mind in bed, but still wakes up early every Sunday to cook breakfast before church. We start to throw out the pieces of our lists that give into our needs as we only care if we feel good.

The crazy part about this is, sometimes it's not even about them making us feel good, but the knowledge that we have them. When we start looking for someone who is everything we ever wanted, there has to be a mention of why we want this type of person.

Why would you want someone who is everything you ever wanted? It makes you feel secure in your choice, I admit that. But the stronger desire is for everyone to see what you're capable of. To see the raised eyebrow of respect when they see how beautiful our wife is. To hear that "Oh... that's you?" Or the head nod in appreciation when the home girls know what your man can do once the kiddos get to bed. To know that bank account is looking good every time you check it. We want them because we believe we deserve them, and we crave the looks and words of others when they appraise our catch.

For some, this may be all they desire. They want someone to get their functionality to an equilibrium. Some just need someone to look good at their elbow or to pop out their heirs to continue the family legacy. I apologize to those kinds of people reading this book now. You picked up the wrong book. While this may be all that's wanted, a marriage should be much more than just basic desires.

But how can we change that? How do we find someone we want, yet someone who is more than just codependent? The easiest way to get rid of a problem is to avoid it and the quickest way to avoid getting something our eyes want and not our hearts is to change the role of the job being applied for.

In blunt words, the prize in the race for love is someone we see as the most beneficial for our lives; someone we can build with, who helps nurture us to be the best version of ourselves without giving up pieces of either party. Someone who accepts us as the individual we are, and in turn, we can trust them as the one we love.

Of course, the desires we want will go into what makes our lives beneficial, but we shouldn't hold them as our first priority. While this person will allow us to get to the levels of growth that we might not have gotten to by our own accord, we are still complete in our own selves.

This is the greatest desire in a romantic relationship, and while it takes us all different times to get to this realization, the red flags in our lives blossom when we realize this basic need isn't the priority we were looking for when we started accepting interviews. The girl who all the homies want may not always be the person who'll listen to you when you're going through hard times.

We spend many a moon trying to see where we went wrong when we look back. When we go over the resume and think over the interview, we look for any red flags we may have missed. Sometimes, the biggest problem is the simplest: The person we hired for the job wasn't what we were looking for.

Imagine looking for a carpenter to add an extra room to your house. You've spent thousands of dollars on this project, and once it's done, you go and check out the specks. At first, you're happy when you got your new room. And as soon as you're about to praise the carpenter, you notice something's off.

Yeah, the hardwood floors look amazing but the light switch won't turn on. So, you call the carpenter, complaining and asking why there's no light in the newest addition to the house. Of course, you're angry, and you spend most of the rant wondering why he could miss such a big problem. The carpenter listens for a while and states simply, "I'm not an electrician. Why didn't you hire one?"

At first, it could seem like the carpenter is being a smart aleck, and I can't blame you if you feel that way. But you can't blame him. He's right. The reason you are lacking running electricity is because you didn't look for someone who could take care of that for you.

And so, on this journey, we're gonna talk about getting the spouse you desire with your heart, and not just the one that looks good for the stomach or eyes. You need someone who is going to be beneficial, and not just someone who makes you feel good.

Dating and "Where are You?"

We live in a world of clicks and likes more than understanding and connections. Our technologically based society makes it extremely easy to cherry-pick people to be the best we want for our lives. So easy in fact, it's almost expected to tell a little white lie somewhere in the courting phase of dating.

Dating sites and social media allow us to easily fall in love with the most superficial version of someone. Not only that, the distance between our heart and our phone allows us to put out the most exaggerated version of ourselves. It's common knowledge that we want to put out the best version of ourselves for the social auction.

Sometimes, it may even appear as if you're dating a representative of the person you want as your spouse for the beginning of the relationship. Think about how much longer you could be dating a representative if you've never met the person in real life. I am, by no means, saying that everyone online is lying to you, but it's also true that the possibility of it happening is high.

Why is there always that urge to hide something online? We all know we don't have to be ourselves online. While we all begin our journey with the desire to stay true to our core selves, we all have been tempted to tell a white lie about ourselves; one that won't be realized until those we're searching for have already taken our bait. (Just a hint ladies: no man that says he's 5'11" online is actually that height. A man that tall will just say he's six feet.)

The temptation to show off the person we want to be will have us trying to hide any fault we find in ourselves. And in our desperation to acquire that sweet thing called love, we lie to ourselves to say that no one else is onto that trick but us.

And honestly, most people who tell white lies

online aren't doing so in a malicious manner. It's done to protect themselves, to stray from that V-word we're so afraid of. No, not vengeance, but VULNERABILITY. We're all hesitant to accept the fact that dating requires vulnerability, because, at the end of the day, we all take measures to avoid pain. But that vulnerability is something we have to give in to. We have to be vulnerable enough, to tell the truth about ourselves.

Some truth about ourselves is easier to tell. That we snore if we sleep on our left side could even be one of the many quips about us that we bring up. But our tongue may be tied when it's time to talk about the nitty-gritty that makes us who we are. The fact that we're going into this altercation, believing our spouse is going to love us until they see all of us may not be something we bring up before, or even after, that big "I do."

But what stops us from being vulnerable with others? There's a lot more at stake than merely us not wanting them to judge us. The loathing of vulnerability we all share is also something we try our hardest to hide. The inability to talk about something typically stems from our loath to accept it. To confidently tell someone about ourselves, we have to understand it as a truth about ourselves.

For us to really see what we have to offer, and what

we are truly looking for in terms of dating and marriage, we have to ask ourselves the question we spend much time avoiding. Humanity has spent so long avoiding answering this question: How do I know? It's the first question in the Bible.

Genesis 3:9 (NASB), Then the LORD God called to the man, and said to him, "Where are you?"

Think about this... When God asked this, He wasn't asking for His sake, but rather for the person whom the question is asked. The question is for you. Check this out, God doesn't ask questions if there is not a reason. Ever since God gave us free will, He has been questioning us not for His sake, but for us to find the questions toward the right path. We learn by putting all of the possible outcomes and/or identifying all of the factors of circumstance into the occasions.

Think about the question, "Where are you?"

What's interesting about this question is that it was not a question God needed to know. Adam was the one who needed to hear the question. The fact of the matter is that Adam knew exactly where he was; or did he? Might I suggest to you that, just like God needed Adam to know where he was, we need to know where we are in our own lives.

Do you know the answer?

When we ask ourselves this question, we're not meant to look up and around us. It's not just a question of physical location, but we treat it like it is. You know where you are at this very moment, at least where your body is. But do you know where you are mentally? Do you know your limits when it comes to the things you have to deal with daily?

Where are you emotionally? Do you know how far you are on that healing journey? Are there still any triggers you might hold off for none to see, not even you? Do you fully understand your financial situation as it is, and not just where you would like it to be? Do you know where you are in your life in response to your goals and purpose? Are these the questions you can answer readily or do you need a few minutes before we continue?

In life, we have to know where we are, lest we find something that tries to lead us down a path we've already taken. There's no point in entering a relationship only to realize months down that you are now trying to stay away from the same partner.

THINK ON THIS!

1. Our hearts are the most precious things about being human, and we don't want to give that treasure over to just anyone.

2. Many problems that arise in looking for someone are rooted in defining the role you're looking for.

3. The reason we take the time to acknowledge ourselves, our past, and our desires before we enter the dating life is so we can easier accept the fact that we are indeed whole.

4. A marriage should be much more than just basic desires. You need someone who is going to be beneficial, and not just the one that looks good for the stomach or eyes or makes you feel good.

5. The prize in the race for love is someone we see as the most beneficial for our lives; someone we can build with, who helps nurture us to be the best version of ourselves without giving up pieces of either party.

6. The girl who all the homies want may not always be the person who'll listen to you when you're going through hard times.

7. Dating sites and social media allow us to easily fall in love with the most superficial version of someone. Sometimes, it may even appear as if we're dating a representative of the person we want as our spouse for the beginning of the relationship.

8. The temptation to show off the person we want to be will have us trying to hide any fault we find in ourselves.

9. We're all hesitant to accept the fact that dating requires vulnerability. But that vulnerability is something we have to give in to. We have to be vulnerable enough, to tell the truth about ourselves.

10. To confidently tell someone about ourselves, we have to understand it as a truth about ourselves.

4

CREDIT AND OTHER THINGS

>
> **DATING IS THE PROCESS BETWEEN BEING SINGLE AND MARRIED, WHICH IS WHY YOU HAVE TO KNOW WHAT YOU WANT OUT OF A PERSON, WHAT YOU WANT OUT OF DATING, AND WHAT YOU INTEND TO HAVE IN A MARRIAGE."

Have you ever tried to use a map to get somewhere without knowing your current destination? No matter what our individual goals are in life, they all fall under the same theme: to be better than who we were.

We all wish to put ourselves in positions that allow us to bloom and prosper. None of us wants to go to a place we had to crawl out of once before. And though this is something we agree with, a lot of us seem to make the pursuit of romantic love the exception to this rule.

—Mike Dean: Grown & Alone...page 40

When dating, the future is as important as the present. We don't start healthy relationships with an end date in mind, rather we expect to be with this person in whatever future we have envisioned ourselves in.

The physical acts of dating may take up only a fraction of our day. The amount of time on our hearts is a much longer and complex slice of time. You're about to share your life with someone, how do you feel about the co-signer?

Have you ever tried to get your parents or another relative to co-sign something for you? If you were the one requesting the co-sign, you might have noticed there was a little bit of hesitation when the question came up.

Maybe you found your dream car, or you've decided to move out but needed help a little, that is, more help getting into that nice apartment. You might even have to ask multiple people until you find someone who finally agrees to help.

Or maybe you were the one hesitating, and you had to hesitate as you pondered co-signing. Or maybe there was no hesitation, but just a flat out rejection. No matter how much love you might have for that person, you didn't want them tied to your credit.

Most people don't hear about credit until their first big purchase. It's not taught much in school, and so the first time we heard the word credit was sitting next to the person we expect to cosign for us. And that's before we even understand what cosigning really means.

We might not understand why we need someone else to show we'll turn the payments in on time or why our word is not good enough. But the expected cosigner-to-be has had years before us thinking in terms of credit. They've spent a lot of time building their credit and making up for mistakes their younger selves made, and they don't want someone's negligence to pull them back into a hole they've gotten themselves out of.

They know their credit history, and they never have to wonder if they will miss a payment because they've felt the consequences before. But as a person who doesn't understand the worth of good credit, there's no need to question whether we'll get what we want.

When we're looking for the person we want to give a slice of our lives to, we must look at their credit. Credit is how much a company should trust that you will do what you will need to do in terms of payment.

Now, credit in the dating world has more to do than just making payments on time. Though finance may not be the most important part of dating credit, both terms have to be a theme in common. Your credit isn't about your ability to perform right now, but your ability to consistently do what you said you could do.

A wise woman once told me: "You never date looking for where you are, but looking for where you're going to be." Why is that? We spend so much time anxious about our future anyway, do we really need to add dating in the midst? Isn't love supposed to be about living in the moment? At many times, yes. But no one makes plans in their lives expecting to relive the same day every day. We don't plan to get a bigger house so we can do the same things we did in our apartment.

Every day we live, we make an effort to be more than we were before. To do that with the wonderful world of dating, you have to know what you have to consistently offer. Though it seems tenacious to give someone a credit score on their lives, your heart is a treasure that should never be taken lightly. You have to think of the growth of the person you wish to be in your life. Once you've found someone you wish to be with, you have to ask yourself questions like this:

How mature do they appear to be emotionally and mentally?

If I choose to become one with them, will they be beneficial in my getting to where I want to be in life?

Is there a chance that this person will hinder the goals I have for my own life?

It gets harder to answer these questions about someone else if you're worried about what it will be like if the script is flipped. If we don't know where we stand on our credit as an adult and spouse, we should run away from asking the question for anyone else's sake. We don't like to see how we hold up, which is why we have to be the first person to do it.

Now, in terms of paying off a car, credit is gained after successfully paying off before the deadline so consistently. But in terms of inviting someone into your heart and life, their credit stands on if they can consistently be the person they said they were. We expect them to be the kind, loving, and caring person that they said they were when we co-signed our hearts with them. There's a certain level of trust that goes into believing they will come through in the manner they say they will.

But they are not using our credit to buy just love, so our credit comes into play in the exchange of happiness and peace.

This is why I repeat in saying you have to know where you are starting in a relationship before you look for a destination with someone else.

It is very important to be happy single before you are happy dating or married. You are asking for trouble entering into a relationship when not being happy and/or choosing someone who is not happy. And by happy, I don't mean someone who doesn't have bad days: If you are looking for that, you'd never find a soul.

You need someone who is content with their life, and if not content, finding ways to accomplish what they are looking for. You don't want someone's bad credit to bring you down or back to a position in the life you had escaped.

We have to remember at times, dating is not just a game to pass the time. Dating is the process between being single and married, which is why you have to know what you want out of a person, what you want out of dating, and what you intend to have in a marriage.

After someone has caught our eye and we've spent enough time with them to see them as a reoccurring face, we no longer simply consider slicing out time to spend alone with them. As we grow closer to the one we call our boo, we start wanting more ways to integrate their presence into our lives.

One of the important factors we use while dating is trying to see if the person we wish to spend our lives with fits into our lifestyle. We don't want them just to be a nice fit in the life we're currently living, but the lifestyle we're building towards as well.

Lifestyle

Before we get too far into the lifestyle part of dating, I will like to acknowledge the elephant in the room. Of course, everyone is expected to change their lifestyles a little when they're in a relationship. Most of us assume it's only natural we should tweak out the "single activities" of our lives. With that being said, it's not all that will probably find a partner that wants them out in the club every night. Relationships are a give and take, and we have to be willing to sacrifice as much as we expect our partners to sacrifice. But when I speak of our lifestyles, it's not just what we do from 9-to-5 and what we use to entertain ourselves on the weekend.

We have to find someone who understands what we're living for. Someone who sees our dreams and aspirations with respect. Someone who understands our beliefs and work schedule, and treats all aspects of our lives with respect.

Of course, it can be hard to believe someone we just met. So, what do we do? We invite them to things that are important to us. We let them see our work, friends, and go out to see movies that mean a lot to us.

That's great.

But when was the last time you went on a date and let your beliefs and priorities be known? In today's society, it's almost a taboo to speak about your beliefs on the first day. You're supposed to get to know them, but not enough to push them away or freak them out: Which is wrong within itself.

If the person you wish to spend your life with doesn't align with your priorities at the beginning of the relationship, what makes you believe they'll have an epiphany further down the relationship? We all want someone in our lifestyle, but we must remember our lifestyle is our system of beliefs, priorities, and purpose in this thing we call life. I can take all of my friends to the movies, that doesn't mean they deserve a ring the moment the credits roll.

To truly know that someone believes you're important to them, you have to see how they handle the things that are important to you.

Have you ever known a woman who convinced a man to go to church with her, only to have their wedding by the last time you see him in the sanctuary? Or a man whose wife shrugs off his aspirations in life, so he spends time speaking to others about what's important to him because he no longer believes his wife cares?

When you're looking for someone who accepts your lifestyle, it's important to see the difference between someone who is doing something with you to get you, and someone who is doing something because it's important to you. This is where credit rears its head again.

The consistency of the relationship may start to change after a few months or years. You start to believe you were wrong because the things you trusted them to do now and in the future is not being seen anymore. No longer do they seem tolerant and loving, but now they may seem distant, bored, and apprehensive. The thing is, most of us show our true selves sooner or later, but it's easy to miss if you're wearing glasses made not to focus on red.

Rose-colored glasses

Well, with that said, we have to be vigilant not to lose ourselves in this race for love. When I say to find someone compatible with your lifestyle, I do not mean to give up the things that are important to you. You should never give up the things that matter to you because you're so ready to be in love again. Sometimes, it's good to evaluate where you think you stand in the compromise section of your relationship; not to see if you're getting everything you think you deserve but to make sure your bends are not done out of fear.

We speak about love, and sometimes forget to acknowledge that we all haven't grown up with the same sense of love. Some of us were raised on a twisted sense of love. We can only give out the things we hold inside of us, so if we were raised on twisted love, if we hadn't learned a better way of living, we would only be able to give others twisted love.

And it has to do a lot with the way we were brought up. There are those of us who weren't raised in love, that is, we were raised in survival. And the attention of another person may cause us to give in to things we were not ready for.

Those who were raised on survival may not react the same way when they're handed genuine, authentic love; so, they look for a love that feels familiar to them.

Going into the world of dating, looking only for what feels right could give way to looking at our partner with rose-colored glasses, since we've finally found what we think we need in order to function in this world.

What do I mean by rose-colored glasses? Well, imagine for a second you bought glasses that had a red tint on them. Wherever you look, you will see red. So, when you look at something that was already red, the red hue wouldn't pop out as much as it would if there was no tint in your line of vision.

The red flags in a relationship, through those rose-colored glasses, just seem like ordinary flags and not the warnings they really are.

It's hard for us to act like someone else all hours of the day. And in the beginning of a relationship, people tend to do just that, showing you the part of them they believe you want to see. But never put on rose-colored glasses because you wish to find love.

Remember, you are a child of God. You deserve love in the purest of forms, which is easy to say, but after a long time of not finding the love you believe you deserve, you start to knock off things trying to find anyone who will take the bait. Those of us who were raised on love may find it easier to align with this idea of not settling. But those of us raised on survival? It's another story altogether.

Being raised on survival makes it easier to forgive our partner for cheating earlier in the relationship because we don't want them to leave. Being raised on survival allows us to stay silent when abuse happens, and to make exceptions for actions that are in no way permissible.

Why?

Because the lack of love in the past tries to force us into submitting to the crumbs of tainted love. If we do not acknowledge the wrongs in the way we were raised, we'll initially start every relationship with rose-colored glasses because we're looking for something familiar. We're looking for something we've seen before, so we know how to react when it comes around the corner. Because at that point, we're not looking for the love we deserve. We're looking for a love that reinforces the negativity we were raised on.

And all of this makes up, again, to the lifestyle you are wishing to bring another soul into. I say this not to judge anyone, as I am not powerful enough to judge anyone. I say this for your own sake.

Your lifestyle is much more than just your day-to-day activities. Your lifestyle includes your beliefs, and all the things you believe are permissible in a relationship.

Acknowledge the past, as it is the only way to go through it, but never allow your desire for love to allow you to go back to your past. You are a new person, and you deserve love in all its aspects.

You deserve the love you're afraid to think about but when you're alone with your heart and your daydreams. You deserve a love worth waiting for, but we'll never accept that we can acquire it until we see that we deserve it. And so, after many a trial and error, you finally find someone who just clicks with you. They work well with the friends and they seem to have their heads on their shoulders. You're happy, everyone around you knows you're on the market. You might even make it social media official.

So, after all this time looking for the next other half, it's time to take things a little further. The next step in dating is the one that causes the most laughs and the one we're most hesitant of...
You guessed it, it's time to meet the family.

THINK ON THIS!

1. You have to know where you are starting in a relationship before you look for a destination with someone else.

2. When dating, the future is as important as the present. We don't start healthy relationships with an end date in mind.

3. Though finance may not be the most important part of dating credit, both terms have to be a theme in common. Your credit isn't about your ability to perform right now, but your ability to consistently do what you said you could do.

4. Though it seems tenacious to give someone a credit score on their lives, your heart is a treasure that should never be taken lightly. You have to think of the growth of the person you wish to be in your life.

5. In terms of inviting someone into your heart and life, their credit stands on if they can consistently be the person they said they were.

6. It is very important to be happy single before you are happy dating or married. You are asking for trouble entering into a relationship when not being happy and/or choosing someone who is not happy.

7. Dating is the process between being single and married, which is why you have to know what you want out of a person, what you want out of dating, and what you intend to have in a marriage.

8. Relationships are a give and take, and we have to be willing to sacrifice as much as we expect our partners to sacrifice.

9. We have to find someone who understands what we're living for. Someone who sees our dreams and aspirations with respect. Someone who understands our beliefs and work schedule, and treats all aspects of our lives with respect.

10. If the person you wish to spend your life with doesn't align with your priorities at the beginning of the relationship, what makes you believe they'll have an epiphany further down the relationship?

THINK ON THIS!

11. To truly know that someone believes you're important to them, you have to see how they handle the things that are important to you.

12. When you're looking for someone who accepts your lifestyle, it's important to see the difference between someone who is doing something with you to get you, and someone who is doing something because it's important to you.

13. We speak about love, and sometimes forget to acknowledge that we all haven't grown up with the same sense of love.

14. Acknowledge the past, as it is the only way to go through it, but never allow your desire for love to allow you to go back to your past.

5
MEETING THE FAMILY

> *A PIECE OF MEDEA-TYPE WISDOM TELLS US THIS: HOW A MAN TREATS HIS MOTHER WILL ALWAYS SHOW HOW HE'LL TREAT YOU. WATCHING HOW YOUR PARTNER INTERACTS WITH THEIR FAMILY IS A GREAT INDICATOR OF HOW THEY'LL REACT TO YOU ONCE THEY'RE TRULY COMFORTABLE WITH YOU."*

Meeting the family is, perhaps, one of the most critical steps in dating. Not only is it essential, but it says I want to bring you into the most sacred part of my life, and that's my family. This also allows you to see how your partner responds in the "Lions Den."

Meeting the family is a steeple to any relationship. It's near impossible to have a long-lasting relationship without both parties mingling with the kin. Honestly, if it's been three months and you don't even know what their parents look like,

I'd advise you to run, take this book with you though.

Most of us either have or heard stories about when meeting the family becomes a little more than just an awkward situation. Seven times out of ten, our "meeting the fam" stories can either be told on a comedy stage or at a therapist's chair. It's one of the few times we're not anxious because we don't know how things will work out, but afraid because we know what could happen.

We know our family, and family tends to go up the antics when we announce a new person is coming over. And it's hard to get mad at them, because we would do the same thing if the positions were reversed.

The intentions are always in the good place, yet it still brings a sliver of ice down our throats at the thought of it. But whether you believe you'll tell your story behind a mic or in front of a psychologist, you have to bite the bullet and bring them around to meet the family. You might laugh, you might cry, but you never can run away from doing it.

With all your faults, your family has seen you through almost every stage of life. They know your highs and your lows, and the truths that you may have a hard time digesting. They know the real you. The probability that they're looking at the new candidate for the love of your life with rose-colored glasses is low.

In layman's terms, your family will be able to see through the bull much better than you would, as they're not the ones falling in love. They're less likely to buy any snake oil that's being sold. They'll always be there to pick up the pieces if you get heartbroken, but they know they're not in the crossfire of heartbreak, which makes it easier for them to evaluate (or judge, depending on how you look at it).

The compatibility between your family and your partner is important for your own peace of mind. It's hard to stay in a long-lasting relationship if the relationship isn't compatible with the relationships you maintain with your family. The stress caused between a relative and your partner butting heads is something we'd all like to avoid, especially if at any point we feel we have to choose sides.

The question we ask ourselves when we think of bringing our partner to our family isn't about our family members looking out for our best interest, but try as we might to remember we are grown and make our own decisions. The question we ask ourselves is, "What if they don't like them?"

At this point, you have to ask yourself why they wouldn't like your partner:

Does my partner treat me in the way I was raised to be treated?

Could their dislike come from the idea that I might be settling?

Does the dislike come from a family member who has my best interest in mind?

Because we can't choose our family (trust many of us have tried), their opinion of our partner must be taken with a grain of salt. Unfortunately, the way of the world does not support that every family member we have will always have our best interest in mind.

You could come home with the greatest apple that fell from the tree only to hear you should have gotten a peach. And we can't lie that sometimes, misery loves company. The dislike they have toward your partner just may be from the fact that they can see you're happier now. We all know the feeling of wanting someone whose opinion means a lot to us, shrivel because they don't want us to do better than them in life.

Meeting the family will be difficult if you're not going to momma's house with a game plan. Your family is going to evaluate your partner whether you want them to or not. I promise, your family will never run out of reason or time to evaluate what you are doing with your life. Constructive criticism from the family can be expected more than rain during the spring, but it's a time to use that to your advantage.

Now, I wouldn't recommend bringing your partner over for the first time during Thanksgiving Dinner because then, you're just asking for trouble. I would hold off from bringing in someone new to any situation where tensions are already running high.

For the love of all things holy, don't bring your new boo over as a buffer, the fam could find a way to buffer them out of your life.

The greatest results come from easing the relationship into the family. The easiest way is to have them meet the parents first. Before you allow them to meet any member of the family, you have to ask yourself if you're doing so for their opinion or their approval.

If their approval is what you're looking for... just take a breather real quick and remind yourself you are indeed a grown adult. Your life decisions shouldn't hinge on the idea of your parents' approval just to hear them say, good job.

You have to fight the urge to slip into a child's place when you go back to your parent's house. This isn't finding a stray cat when you were little and asking them if you can keep it. I say this because dating is the process between being single and married. With that said, it's the process in which you leave your mother and father to become one with another partner.

Meeting the family is much more important than hearing 'Good job,' as they come with you right up until you walk down that aisle. It's about giving them a glimpse into the part of your life you can't always have them ready on standby for. It's a showing of "This is the next step." And not "Is it okay if I make this next step?"

If your parents have failed to run your partner off, good job, now it's time to meet the ones whose lips may be a little looser when it comes to what they think of your new boo. The trade-off here is this:

even though the rest of the family may have more opinions about your new boo than your parents, once you've handled the parents, everything else seems easier in comparison. (Now Grandma may be a different story altogether but we're gonna have to handle that on an individual basis).

As mentioned before, when meeting the rest of the family, it's more about seeing how your partner handles those you've grown up with rather than their approval. You can watch out for any red flags you may come across when everyone is together. Though, I may suggest waiting until your boo isn't around before you ask them what they think. Family is sure to turn that conversation into a game of Family Feud if you're not careful.

Going With Your Partner to See Their Family

Once your family has roasted you enough, and you have decided in your relationship it's time to return the favor, remember there is a slight agenda into meeting their family. It's one thing to hide your true self around your friends. It's another thing altogether not to be yourself around your family. And watching how your partner interacts with their family is a great indicator of how they'll react to you once they're truly comfortable with you.

A piece of Medea-type wisdom tells us this: how a man treats his mother will always show how he'll treat you. If you're really in this relationship for the long run, it's important to see how they act around the people who've had the longest run with them. While it's important to enjoy yourself around the new candidates for in-laws, use this time to understand your partner on a deeper level.

Remember to be yourself; you are not a stray cat. This isn't a session to prove your worth to your partner's parents. This is a moment to figure out what to expect in the long run. Don't be afraid to ask questions, such as what your partner was like when they were younger. Most parents will be delighted at the chance to embarrass their child.

I'm not saying you should treat it like an interview, but it is important to learn what to expect. You can remember from your own family, taking the time to outdo each other, to give and obtain too much information; this is a great time to see each other without the veil.

As we all know, marrying someone isn't just marrying them, but the family as well. However, certain family members deserve their own plan when it comes to meeting someone new. Meeting the parents is easy, but meeting the children? Well...

THINK ON THIS!

1. The compatibility between your family and your partner is important for your own peace of mind. It's hard to stay in a long-lasting relationship if the relationship isn't compatible with the relationships you maintain with your family.

2. Your family will be able to see through the bull much better than you would, as they're not the ones falling in love.

3. Meeting the family will be difficult if you're not going to momma's house with a game plan.

4. Constructive criticism from the family can be expected more than rain during the spring, but use that to your advantage.

5. For the love of all things holy, don't bring your new boo over as a buffer, the fam could find a way to buffer them out of your life.

6. Before you allow your partner to meet any member of your family, you have to ask yourself if you're doing so for their opinion or their approval.

7. You have to fight the urge to slip into a child's place when you go back to your parent's house.

8. Even though the rest of the family may have more opinions about your new boo than your parents, once you've handled the parents, everything else seems easier in comparison.

9. A piece of Medea-type wisdom tells us this: how a man treats his mother will always show how he'll treat you. Watching how your partner interacts with their family is a great indicator of how they'll react to you once they're truly comfortable with you.

10. As we all know, marrying someone isn't just marrying them, but the family as well.

6

(S)HE GOT KIDS

IF YOU FEEL YOU'RE NOT PREPARED TO BE WITH SOMEONE WHO HAS KIDS, BE APPRECIATIVE OF THEIR TIME AND TELL THEM UPFRONT."

Meeting parents, uncles and aunties, and cousins is one thing. Meeting 'children' is another thing altogether.

One of the reasons we put so much emphasis on meeting kids is our responsibility for our kids. We don't bring anyone to our parents with the understanding we have to protect our parents. Our parents are not our responsibility. But our children? Every aspect of their lives is vetted to ensure they are safe and protected, and that they feel secure with whomever we've placed in their surroundings.

—Mike Dean: Grown & Alone...page 68

We all have mixed feelings on the appropriate time to bring talk about kids in the dating process. Too late, and your partner feels bombarded with prevarication. But what is too soon to tell someone we have little ones depending on us? We keep our kids close to us, not giving out information to just about anyone.

There's also another reason we worry about when to speak of our little ones. In our society, dating with children has a turn of being seen as, "I've tried this before and it didn't work."

Society has long alluded a bad connotation when it comes to dating someone who has kids. Instead of treating the children like the blessings they are, our society has found a way to deem them as nothing more than trophies from failed relationships. When we see children as baggage, we create a wall between them and us that they never asked for and didn't deserve.

If you're dating someone who has children, you must be aware of the fact that they are a package deal. There's no way you can have their parent in your life without accepting the children as well. As much as it sucks, you have to ask yourself if you are prepared and mature enough to have children in your life. You must accept that at one point you will spend time with the family, and not just your partner.

You have to understand that even if you believe you have an envied position in your partner's life, their children will come first. It takes a rather mature person to understand they will not be the first priority in their spouse's eyes. Are you okay with playing second place to little ones? Can you understand that, at times, plans may be cancelled in order to take care of the children?

We all understand that dating is the bridge between being single and being married. Do you believe you'd be a good step-parent? Will you be able to understand that at a certain point, children who have no biological ties to you will look up to you for support, understanding, and companionship? Can you understand that because of the children, you will be tied to the other parent as long as you wish a loving relationship with their partner?

This may sound like scare propaganda stopping you from being a step-parent, or at the very least, a campaign against dating someone with children. I can assure you, I'm not here to scare anyone intentionally. If the series of questions left a bad taste in your mouth, you may want to ask yourself if you're prepared for this line of dating, because, these are questions you have to ask yourself.

The desire to push away from these questions may show a lack of desire. If you see children as baggage, you have a little while to go before you're ready for this level of commitment. You have to understand your actions are not just tied into you and your spouse, but the little ones as well. Communication is key, and if you're ready to take this next step, by all means. But if you feel you're not prepared to be with someone who has kids, be appreciative of their time and tell them upfront.

If you are the partner with children, the question of when to let your partner meet your children becomes a pivotal part of your dating experience. There's no way to separate your dating life from your children, as each part of your life affects them in some way. The trickle-down economics of your life will always be in the back of your mind, whether you're a single mother or father. There is no formula that I can use to tell you when to let them meet your children, because it's your life that you have to put in consideration, not mine. It's your children you're worried about, so everything has to be viewed on an individual purpose.

If you're looking for short-term dating and thrills, you may honestly see no reason to bring your children up in your dating life. But if you're looking for long term, you have to think not only about how your partner will be a wife/husband to you, but a parent to your children.

Here are some questions you'll have to ask yourself:

1. How does my partner react when I bring up the issue of my kids?

2. Do they seem like a person I can trust with my kids when I'm around?

3. How about when I'm not around?

We have to talk about the other parent, too. It is the adult thing to let the mother/father of your children know when you decide to bring another adult into their children's life. But this is done for the sake of the children, not to show off you've found someone better. A lot of repressed emotions can show up in this part of your relationships, and tensions can appear if each party isn't open and honest with themselves. We all know stories of ex-partners becoming bitter because someone has decided to bring someone new into their hearts. This is why I say you have to heal from your other relationships first. The last romantic relationship is dead, yes, but the care and concern are still there. The need to look after the children is still there, and once children are involved, we have to let go of the selfishness we had before. Communicate, but make sure everything you're doing is coming from a place of concern and care, and not a place of showing off. How you treat their other parent will always come up later in life, good or bad.

There is an irony of having children though. We understand how important they are. We know they hold a position in our lives that no adult can replace or replicate. But as their parent, we sometimes forget we are not omnipotent.

Our children look at us sometimes like we're superheroes, whereas, in reality, we have very little idea if we're doing everything correctly all the time. We understand our children's power but sometimes forget they have their own opinions.

Once you've introduced your children to your partner, don't forget to ask them how they feel about your new partner. Nine times out of ten, children are smarter and more observant than we give them credit for.

It does no one good to assume how your children feel about your new partner. You are attempting to change their lives every time you put forth an effort to change yours. So, we have to be open and honest with our children. As much as we try our best to shelter them and protect them, it's easy to fall into the assumption that nothing is wrong.

Talk to them, as they're human and they will always let you know how they feel. The good thing about children is, they like to tell you too much once they get the ball rolling.

Now, anyone with children will know children aren't the candidates for being gung-ho about change. Resistance should be expected, as your children may feel you're trying to replace their other parent. They may put up a fight. Tantrums around your new partner can be expected during the first part of them being around. But if there is love in all aspects of this relationship, each relationship will blossom and grow.

THINK ON THIS!

1. We all have mixed feelings on the appropriate time to bring talk about kids in the dating process. But what is too soon to tell someone we have little ones depending on us?

2. When we see children as baggage, we create a wall between them and us that they never asked for and didn't deserve.

3. When children are involved, it takes a rather mature person to understand they will not be the first priority in their spouse's eyes.

4. If you feel you're not prepared to be with someone who has kids, be appreciative of their time and tell them upfront.

5. It is the adult thing to let the mother/father of your children know when you decide to bring another adult into their children's life.

6. Our children look at us sometimes like we're superheroes, whereas, in reality, we have very little idea if we're doing everything correctly all the time.

7. Nine times out of ten, children are smarter and more observant than we give them credit for.

7
S.E.X

> *IF YOU TAKE SEX OUT FROM THE RELATIONSHIP, YOU SEE WHO'S THERE IN ORDER TO BUILD WITH YOU. YOU CAN SEE WHO WANTS TO HAVE A RELATIONSHIP AND WHO ONLY DOES RELATIONSHIP THINGS FOR THE TREAT."*

We're all adults here, and so we will talk about sex like adults do. It's wonderful. We all look forward to the surge of oxytocin, serotonin, and dopamine that comes with it.

Sex is being thrown in our faces the moment we turn on the television or go onto social media. We know it sells, it grabs our attention, and a vast majority of dating in recent years has become looking for someone to regularly and exclusively have sex with. I advise everyone to wait until marriage before crossing that bridge, and that's not just because of the vows I took when I became a pastor.

Sex is everywhere in our society. Nothing holds our eyes quite like it, which is why we see it in everything from advertisements for soda to social media. But society limits its talk of sex to its biological, chemical, and social sense. We speak of sex so much because of how nice it feels. But rarely in society do we talk about all the things that come along with sex.

Society treats sex as a conquest: he who has the biggest body counts wins. Now we all know the dangers of sex, especially the unprotected kind. We are taught to protect our bodies from sexually transmitted diseases. We are taught to protect our bank accounts from unplanned pregnancies. But we shy away from speaking about protecting our souls and spirits from ties we do not need.

We rarely talk about soul ties in society. And I believe the reason we steer clear from this aspect is the sense of guilt we have when we speak of soul ties. When we lay with someone, for that duration, we become one with them. A piece of us ties to them and a piece of them with us. Now, if you've thought of everyone you've had sex with, are you happy to know you have a piece of them with you? I'll give you a moment to swallow the bile.

There are some of us who are happy with the people we've made soul ties with. There are some who will only acknowledge those soul ties after a few drinks. It's easy to deny those soul ties if you see sex only as a recreational pastime. As with anything we do to "have fun," we try to push down the consequences that could happen if we enjoy our fun a little too much.

Sex is much more than horizontal therapy. There is a reason why we preach on abstinence, and it isn't to spitefully deny you pleasures from the view of our high horses. If you make soul ties with someone who isn't where you need to be, you can find yourself making excuses for the actions you find yourself doing. You can start devolving to a person you used to be without an explanation. Mingling body parts is one thing, what about mingling your soul with a dark soul? Hesitation starts to rear its ugly head, with good reason.

There is a reason why the elders speak about waiting until marriage to have sex, and this reason is more practical. To declare you're waiting to have sex, and holding true to this declaration, allows the weaker ones to wean themselves out.

Sex is one of the great parts of a relationship, and to some, sex is the reward of a relationship. It's the treat for good behavior. Now, if you take that away, you see who's there in order to build with you. You can see who wants to have a relationship and who only does relationship things for the treat. If your partner becomes frustrated because you've decided to wait, they are not there for all the aspects of being in a relationship with you.

Because of the society we live in, sometimes relationships are seen merely as, "you are the only person I will have sex with," and nothing more. But someone who understands your wishes and waits, shows they care more about you than just your body parts.

And I write this chapter for the men too. We're not exempt from this rule. It is not a woman's job to keep us in check. We are to be able to do that on our own accord. The same society that tells women to cover up and be prudent allows us, men, to do whatever we want whenever we want.

We get a pass from society to be as promiscuous as we want, and we are allowed to settle down when that water runs dry. But you are not here simply to listen to what society tells you to do. We have to hold ourselves to a higher degree.

To the men reading this, I ask you this: Is the woman you wish to be your wife important enough for you to deny your little head for as long as it takes?

And if the answer is "No," why are you with her?

Sex Versus Intimacy

While we all look for sex because it feels great, most of us have more desires behind sex than we put into words. It feels good for our body, and the chemical reactions are sought after, but what we're looking for is intimacy.

Intimacy is a need we all have as humans, and it's something we are willing to forgo core beliefs to acquire. We want someone we can feel vulnerable with, someone we can be naked and bare all to. We look for someone we can show ourselves to, warts and all. And when we do this, when we complete this need, our brain rewards us with feel-good chemicals. Our heart flutters to tell us we've made a good decision.

We all seek intimacy, even if we're too afraid to admit it. We want to be able to look at someone being as vulnerable to us as we are to them; someone who shows appreciation to our bareness. Even the most hard-hearted people look for one person to be soft around. But because of our sex-filled world, most of us aren't aware of the other types of intimacy. Even if we know how we want it, if sex is off the table, a few of us would struggle listing ways we could be intimate with our partners.

It is nothing less than tragic to see, but thankfully, we all can be greater than what we were taught. There may be some who see sex as the only way to be intimate with someone, and "no sex before marriage" takes the only tool they have in their arsenal. To them, I give something to rejoice over: God did not make us to be one-dimensional. Of all His creation, human beings exalt in the ability to become anew, to consciously forge another version of themselves.

There are more ways to be intimate than sex, and sometimes the plainer things may be scarier than the more exciting ones. There are more ways to be naked and vulnerable, and the scariest one is communication.

Intimacy is just the act of being close to someone; to know that when you're around them, you can let down the walls the outside world isn't allowed to breakthrough.

Can you speak to your partner about anything that's on your mind? If you want to be held, and nothing more, can you go to them?
Do you feel the need to cower away on your bad days, or can you be vulnerable with them no matter how your headspace that day?

While there must be a timeline on sex when it comes to a relationship, intimacy is something that needs to be there for a relationship to grow. The biggest difference between a romantic relationship and a platonic one is the level of intimacy we expect going into it. We want to hold hands and snuggle, to lay back against someone on the couch, or take baths with. We want to do things that reinforce that this person is for us and with us. But when we speak about intimacy and being close to another human being, we must acknowledge the different love languages we have as people.

THINK ON THIS!

1. We speak of sex so much because of how nice it feels. But rarely in society do we talk about all the things that come along with sex.

2. We are taught to protect our bodies from sexually transmitted diseases. We are taught to protect our bank accounts from unplanned pregnancies. But we shy away from speaking about protecting our souls and spirits from ties we do not need.

3. If you've thought of everyone you've had sex with, are you happy to know you have a piece of them with you?

4. If you make soul ties with someone who isn't where you need to be, you can find yourself making excuses for the actions you find yourself doing.

5. There is a reason why the elders speak about waiting until marriage to have sex, and this reason is more practical. Mingling body parts is one thing, what about mingling your soul with a dark soul?

6. If you take sex out from the relationship, you see who's there in order to build with you. You can see who wants to have a relationship and who only does relationship things for the treat.

7. Men, is the woman you wish to be your wife important enough for you to deny your little head for as long as it takes? If the answer is "No," why are you with her?

8. God did not make us to be one-dimensional. Of all His creation, human beings exalt in the ability to become anew, to consciously forge another version of themselves.

9. While there must be a timeline on sex when it comes to a relationship, intimacy is something that needs to be there for a relationship to grow.

10. If your partner becomes frustrated because you've decided to wait, they are not there for all the aspects of being in a relationship with you.

8
LOVE LANGUAGES

> *COMMUNICATION IS ONE OF THE BIGGEST FACTORS IN A HEALTHY RELATIONSHIP, AND MANY OF THE PROBLEMS IN A RELATIONSHIP COME FROM THE LACK OF COMMUNICATION."*

There may be some of us who have never heard of the term "love language," and so, we're going to speak about them like it's our first time hearing it.

Someone's love language is the way that person feels loved and appreciated the most. Everyone's love language may be a little different than others, but all love languages can be described in five categories:

1. Words of affirmation
2. Acts of service

3. Receiving gifts
4. Quality time
5. Physical touch

A person with a "words of affirmation" love language delights in hearing how much they're loved and appreciated. Things like, "I like your hair today" and "that tie looks nice to you" warms their heart because they like to hear it. Hearing the words "I love you" connects with them higher than just showing them you love them. On the flip side, negative remarks and snide comments may have a heavier weight to those of this love language than others.

Someone with an "acts of service" love language feels most appreciated when things are done for them. A good motto for them can be, "actions speak louder than words." Things such as cooking them a meal, picking up prescriptions, doing laundry, or even taking care of the kids so they can sleep in a little longer go a long way for them. However, actions done in obligation do not hold the same power. This could be seen as a matter of, "I want you to do it because you want to, not because I constantly tell you that you have to."

Those with a "receiving gifts" love language like to receive little tokens of appreciation. This doesn't mean they're asking you to break the bank to show how much you love them. It can be as simple as picking up their favorite candy on the way home from work. Buying them their favorite wine on their birthday. It doesn't mean they're looking at the receipt every time you say, "look what I got you." Just something to show that they were on your mind.

The "quality time" love language doesn't care that much about gifts. The thing they're asking from you the most is to spend time with them. Quality time is something we rarely feel we have in today's day and age, with all the distractions that are always ready at the fingertips. To give your partner quality time means time without constant texting and checking your feed; to spend time without worrying about how many likes you've received, or what's the score on the game at the moment.

This doesn't mean you can't curl up and watch a movie. But someone with a quality time love language likes to know you're spending time with them—not that they're just there when you're relaxing. What that means is, they don't want to feel included in this quality time, but the quality time is meant for them and them alone.

The last love language is physical touch. People with this love language like to feel you're there.

Now that doesn't mean they want French kisses every thirty minutes, but things such as hand-holding, hugging, and kissing mean a lot to them. They want to know you're there with them not just emotionally, but they want to be able to reach out and touch you, and be touched in return.

It doesn't take that long to describe the five love languages. They all are simple enough that anyone can get the jest of what they entail, just by the name of each of them. The frustration comes when there's a misunderstanding between your partner's love language and what you think your partner's love language is. Both parties will become frustrated when you come home with flowers but all they wanted was a long hug when you came in the door. You may have the "words of affirmation" love language, and can't understand why your partner can't just say the words.

Before we get into understanding your partner's love language, are you aware of what category you fall in? Are you someone who likes words of affirmation or physical touch? Are you a mixture of one or two depending on how you feel?

As mentioned before, we are not one-dimension creatures, so it can be a mixture. But we have to be honest with ourselves when we're looking to be appreciated and loved. Are you able to communicate your love language in a way that makes sense? Are you able to tell your partner when you feel your needs are not being met?

What of your partner's? Do you know their love language(s)? Can you tell if they would like a hug more than a new necklace? Or when spending more quality time with them means more than showing you've taken out the trash that day?

Communication is one of the biggest factors in a healthy relationship, and many of the problems in a relationship come from the lack of communication. While understanding your partner, also understand what it takes for them to feel appreciated and loved. Explain to them what your heart desires, so that you can save yourselves a lot of frustration and arguments later.

THINK ON THIS!

1. Communication is one of the biggest factors in a healthy relationship, and many of the problems in a relationship come from the lack of communication.

2. A person with a "words of affirmation" love language delights in hearing how much they're loved and appreciated. Hearing the words "I love you" connects with them higher than just showing them you love them.

3. To give your partner quality time means time without constant texting and checking your feed.

4. Someone with a quality time love language likes to know you're spending time with them—not that they're just there when you're relaxing.

5. Both parties will become frustrated when you come home with flowers but all they wanted was a long hug when you came in the door.

9
THE NEAR AND THE FAR

> *I WON'T TELL ANYONE NOT TO TRY LONG-DISTANCE, BUT I WILL ADVISE YOU NOT TO GET INTO ONE IF YOU DON'T FEEL YOU TRUST YOURSELF OR YOUR PARTNER ENOUGH FOR THE RELATIONSHIP TO LAST."*

We all look at different relationships with different levels of seriousness. Telling a friend that we've started dating again will be taken with a grain of salt. Telling a friend that we let our partner meet our parents will cause them to question if our partner is the one.

There are a few steps, however, in a relationship that call for as much attention or questioning as saying, "We've decided to move in together." These words not only change your relationship but your lifestyle as well.

Today, more people are living together who are just in a relationship than when our grandparents were our age.

Why?

Many reasons would race to show up, but I'll quickly point to two, which are in themselves, potential dangers to a thriving relationship.
The first is what I'd call a relationship of convenience.

A relationship of convenience is exactly how it sounds. The two partners stay in the relationship because it provides the things they need in their lives. Sometimes, that need is affection. Or, the need may just be someone who's around. It might also be that one of the partners needs a place to stay, and the other offers up their living area.

At first, what is convenient will look like God's personal gift because it relieves a problem. So, it may seem grand at the beginning. But after some time, that relationship of convenience becomes a relationship of codependence.

The second reason many people believe in moving in together before marriage is just as a way of testing the waters. Hence, they see moving in as a test run.

Many of those folks believe they can figure their compatibility before they bring vows and the government in the relationship. Studies would show that moving in may be counterintuitive in this sense.

According to a study done by Us Attorney Legal Services, a couple that has not lived together before marriage has a smaller percent chance of divorcing within five years. If the couple has lived together prior to tying the knot, the percentage jumps exponentially.

Beyond all these, what many people don't seem to pay attention to is the fact that moving in together before marriage makes the "no sex before marriage" rule near impossible. We're human, and if you're able to resist that temptation while living with your partner, I would advise you to start hosting classes.

And the Far

When it comes to matters of the heart, we gauge our willingness to do something on our ability to see the outcome in it. Even if the outcome is something we may not necessarily want to see, we are willing to do something about it more than if we can't see how things would plan out.

This lack of control causes us to freak out by the possibility of doing it. Not because we think it will be bad, but because we don't know if it will be bad or not. The biggest area of dating where we feel a mutual lack of control over is long-distance relationships.

Long-distance relationships are one of the many boogeymen in the dating world. We have all heard ghost stories (either from someone we know personally or a secondhand account) of long-distance relationships gone wrong.

The animosity toward LDR's has been around since its conception, and this was before the concept of social media and catfishing. The animosity of LDR's comes from the amount of trust required to be in one. And many of us would not like to give that amount of trust to anyone.

LDR's can be broken into two categories: one that starts at the beginning of a relationship and one that starts in the middle of a relationship. Relationships that start in the beginning as LDR's are typically those that start online; such as through dating sites and social media. LDR's that start in the middle of the relationship are usually caused by a change in lifestyle, such as a new job or a need to move. Both categories have their obstacles, but for now, we are going to talk about the second category.

The reason is, relationships that start as LDR's only have an LDR as a basis for the relationship. Whereas there is a higher level of closeness that comes with an LDR that begins in the middle of a relationship, and that closeness doesn't stop at physical proximity. There is an exchange that goes on with a person you can readily see and be around that doesn't always transfer when more distance is added. A sharing of experiences that we start to long for once we can't see our significant other as much as we used to.

While LDR's aren't inherently bad, the fear that comes along with them is. The fear of them is so intense in some that a relationship will end just because an LDR becomes a possibility. The give and take that comes with agreeing on an LDR is usually seen as this: a decrease in control and an increase in blind loyalty. We think that we're being asked to trust our significant other fully, but we lose many ways we could to verify their words and actions. The biggest fear in an LDR is that our significant other may cheat, or even no longer acknowledge the relationship they are in once they are away from the warden.

Most of this fear comes from stories we've heard about LDR's. We've heard so many bad stories that it's a reflex to assume that underhand things will be happening in the relationship. Some of us are unfortunate enough to have firsthand experience with an LDR going bad.

I won't tell anyone not to try long-distance, but I will inform you that everyone is different, and every situation has its own benefits and cons. I will advise you not to get into one if you don't feel you trust yourself or your partner enough for the relationship to last. If that's the case, it's better to have a little hurt now than a lot of hurt in the future.

There is one type of LDR that I would like to speak about; one that I have witnessed several times: A long-distance relationship with someone in jail. While it carries the concerns of a regular long-distance relationship, it also carries burdens that are brought because of the penial system.

A significant other behind bars is one that cannot help if anything goes wrong; one that cannot be there whenever you wish to talk to them. It also brings the question of whether they will be the same person they were when they come out.

Do you have the patience to put your life on hold

for someone, be it years or even decades? Unless wrongly convicted, you have to ask yourself if the person they are is the person you still want to continue in your life, even as your life progresses. A lot can happen in a matter of years, and the worst thing would be seeing how far the gap of growth is, between you and your significant other.

If you decide that's what you want to do, all power to you. If you believe you deserve something different, then communicate those desires. The last thing we want is someone who spent years anticipating someone only to see they never got their "Dear John" letter.

All in all, Long Distance Relationships are a hurdle within themselves, but with communication and patience, they can make a relationship stronger. Some would prefer to do the traditional relationship strengthening, but to ease their own. The timeframe of a long-distance relationship has a lot to do with how people handle these situations.

THINK ON THIS!

1. There are few steps in a relationship that acquire as much attention or questioning as saying, "We've decided to move in together."

2. After some time, a relationship of convenience becomes a relationship of codependence.

3. The biggest area of dating where we feel a mutual lack of control over is long-distance relationships.

4. The animosity toward LDR's has been around since its conception, and this was before the concept of social media and catfishing.

5. There is an exchange that goes on with a person you can readily see and be around that doesn't always transfer when more distance is added.

6. The biggest fear in an LDR is that our significant other may cheat, or even no longer acknowledge the relationship they are in once they are away from the warden.

7. Long Distance Relationships are a hurdle within themselves, but with communication and patience, they can make a relationship stronger.

8. I won't tell anyone not to try long-distance, but I will advise you not to get into one if you don't feel you trust yourself or your partner enough for the relationship to last.

10

KEEPING GOD FIRST IN YOUR RELATIONSHIP

> **GOD UNDERSTANDS YOUR NEED FOR LOVE. HE UNDERSTANDS THE HEARTBREAK OF NOT GETTING THE LOVE YOU FEEL YOU RIGHTLY DESERVE. THIS IS THE GOD WHO GETS HIS HEART BROKEN CONSTANTLY AND STILL WANTS US TO WANT HIM."**

I know we've spoken over this topic here and there as we went over the different aspects of a love life, but this piece is so important, and I feel we need to speak on it a little more.

As you know, we have to allow God in every aspect of our lives, but sometimes it's hard to give Him His piece in our love life. We are readily giving Him His part in our work life, in our spiritual life (I got questions if you're not allowing Him in your spiritual life), and even transcending to better parts of your lives.

~Mike Dean: Grown & Alone...page 102

When it comes to loving our mother or our sister, we pray and ask God for help and guidance. But we fall short at times when it's time to speak to Him in romantic life. Have you ever wondered why this happens? Why is it a reflex to ask for His guidance at the beginning of finding a partner but you find yourself skipping over that part of your life in your daily prayers? It's due to the most common misconception we have about our Creator: He just wouldn't understand.

It's easy to speak to the Creator of the universe about things we think He'd understand. He tells us how to act toward our family and our neighbors but when we fall in love, we think He's too powerful to understand that emotion; that He is too big to understand heartbreak; or to understand how it feels to want someone so badly and not get that person. I mean, how could He understand?

When was the last time you heard about God downloading Tinder? As humans, we sometimes have this unspoken notion that the God of Love doesn't understand romantic love. And though we don't speak this to others, I promise you others have felt this way; that He has so much more on His plate than matters of the heart.

We find ourselves crying at night wishing the pain

would go away, but keeping it away from Him because he just wouldn't understand. I have made the same mistake until I realize how wrong I was. I'm sure He's been chuckling every time we've thought: "God I'm hurting, but you wouldn't understand what it feels like to want someone so badly."

The funny thing is, we're talking about the author, subject, and sole marketing piece of the longest love letter you will ever read in your life. Many a time we think God wouldn't understand what it means to hurt because we look at the Bible as a set of rules that we have to obey; that we are only here to obey, and if we do a really good job at being the obedient servant He wants us to be, He will allow us into Heaven.

Well, if you see the Bible as an instruction booklet, then it's easy to convey that as, "He wouldn't understand how it feels to be heartbroken." He's the God of Love after all, how in the world could He be lacking in that department?

But when we break it down, the Bible is much more than a "How to Get into Heaven for Dummies." From Genesis to Revelation, God is saying to us, "I want you to love me. I have done all these things for you because I love you, but I want you to love me too. No matter what you do, I'll still ask you to love me. No matter how lost you feel, I still want to be invited into your life. I want to be there because you want me there, not because you feel obligated to. Can't you see how bad I want a relationship with you?! Why can't you see this?!"

Sounds familiar? You might have said the same words as your ex walked out of your life. Imagine saying this to billions of people every day, simply asking to be loved in return. We put God on a (much deserved) pedestal - you know - God of love, Creator of the universe, all-powerful, and all-knowing. And because of that, we place so much distance between Him and us that we neglect to see Him as He appears in our lives.

It's crazy to think about it, but God looks at you like the nerd in high school who does the head cheerleader's homework just to get her to say yes to his prom proposal. We withhold our romantic lives from the One Entity begging us day in and day out, "Please love Me. I'll do anything to show I love you, so please love Me back."

That nagging feeling we're all born with, that "I am worthy of love, so I will give you love and expect love back" comes from the piece of Him that dwells in us. That "I will show you how much

I love you until you see it yourself, and then I'll do more so you never have to question" comes because He's been doing that since Adam and Eve. He understands your need for love. He understands the heartbreak of not getting the love you feel you rightly deserve. This is the God who gets His heart broken constantly and still wants us to want Him.

But it's hard to see this when we see Him and His Word as something merely to follow. It's hard to bring Him into our romantic lives if we don't see His blessings as a way of Courting and His guidance as a declaration of how much He loves and wants us.

We should all be blessed that God isn't as petty as His creation. Could you imagine, withholding this part of love from Him, and Him saying, "Bruh... I've been saying the same words to you since you were born and you have the audacity to say, 'I don't understand?' I would let Michael deal with you since you don't want to listen to me..."

It's laughable, to say the least. We may even feel embarrassed at our own folly. But that's okay, because He isn't as petty as you and me. Never be afraid to bring the God of Love into your search for Love. Come to think of it, if you can't see Him in your relationship, is it really love?

THINK ON THIS!

1. It's easy to speak to the Creator of the universe about things we think He'd understand. He tells us how to act toward our family and our neighbors but when we fall in love, we think He's too powerful to understand that emotion.

2. As humans, we sometimes have this unspoken notion that the God of Love doesn't understand romantic love.

3. The Bible is much more than a "How to Get into Heaven for Dummies." From Genesis to Revelation, God is saying to us, "I have done all these things for you because I love you, but I want you to love me too."

4. We withhold our romantic lives from the One Entity begging us day in and day out, "Please love Me. I'll do anything to show I love you, so please love Me back."

5. We put God on a (much deserved) pedestal – you know - God of love, Creator of the universe, all-powerful, and all-knowing. And because of that, we place so much distance between Him and us that we neglect to see Him as He appears in our lives.

6. God understands your need for love. He understands the heartbreak of not getting the love you feel you rightly deserve. This is the God who gets His heart broken constantly and still wants us to want Him.

7. Never be afraid to bring the God of Love into your search for Love. Come to think of it, if you can't see Him in your relationship, is it really love?

11

IF IT ISN'T LOVE

> **"SOME THINGS ARE MEANT TO BE ACCEPTED WITHOUT CLOSURE OR FULL UNDERSTANDING. AND THAT'S NOTHING AGAINST YOU, THAT'S LIFE ITSELF."**

It would be remiss of me to not speak about the irony of writing a chapter on breakups in a book on dating. Some could even call it counterintuitive. But the very real and disheartening part about the dating world is that breakups happen, and they happen more often than we wish them to.

I wish I could say there was a magical spell we could use in order to make sure the very next relationship will be the one where we finally bring home the gold. But there's not, and even if there was this magical spell to get together with the love of our lives, the spell doesn't let us know how long we'll stay with them. Be it two weeks or twenty years, relationships end all around us.

The amount of time we think about it with our own partner varies, but we all know the feeling. I say this because, if you're reading a book on dating, you probably know how it feels when it doesn't go the way you planned.

Breakups are rough. There's no way around that. Most of the time, immediately after a breakup, we feel broken ourselves. The ending of a relationship has hurt the best of us, be it a separation of a husband from the wife or a boyfriend from the girlfriend, we feel like the world crashed all around us and no one seems to care. We spend time running away from pain and trying to substitute what we lost with sex and other pleasures.

By now, you might not want to try at all in going to find the love of your life. We spent an entire book together, and I waited until toward the end of the book to tell you it might not work?

Well, remember the Title is Grown and Alone, not just Dating 101. And if we're all grown, we all have to be aware of the reality of dating, and we have to understand where we need to go from there.

Breaking up is always seen as the end of dating. It's the game over we never want to see and never want to hear about. None of us like picking up the pieces when our lives do not go the way we planned it, especially if we had spent months and years with the person we love.

Breakups hurt. There's no looking around that, but breakups don't mean life no longer has any meaning. We, with the help of countless movies and dramas, see breaking up as being dropped off into despair of singlehood that none of us asked for and none of us know how to get out of. But just because it feels like this doesn't mean the reality of the situation is following suit. We allow our emotions to get the best of us, especially since they're so raw at this point in our lives, and we start looking at the past in the best rose-colored glasses our psyche can buy.

All breakups end because one party was not being valued as much as they should have been, and both parties agree (if not reluctantly) to part ways. Breakups don't mean there was a problem with either person. Just that the relationship has run its course. And that is something that takes its sweet time to be revealed.

We beat ourselves up to the point that we

internalize every wrong situation in our last relationship, but something we have to learn: to let go. Some things are meant to be accepted without closure or full understanding. And that's nothing against you, that's life itself.

To those who aren't exactly vets in the game of dating... I want to end this piece of advice by bringing up the phrase, "I'll find someone better than you." We've all heard it, thought it, and/or said it at least once in our lives. And this saying is partly true. You will find someone better than your last, but not in the sense of all-around worth and assets. You will find someone better for you than they were, and so will they. And that's okay.

THINK ON THIS!

1. The very real and disheartening part about the dating world is that breakups happen, and they happen more often than we wish them to.

2. Breakups hurt. There's no looking around that, but breakups don't mean life no longer has any meaning.

3. Breakups don't mean there was a problem with either person. Just that the relationship has run its course.

4. Some things are meant to be accepted without closure or full understanding. And that's nothing against you, that's life itself.

12
THAT'S ALL FOLKS

"ALWAYS TAKE THE TIME TO LET YOUR PERSON KNOW YOU SEE BEING WITH THEM AS NOTHING SHORT OF AN ADVENTURE, BECAUSE, WHEN WE SHOW HOW MUCH WE LOVE OTHERS, THEY IN TURN SHOW THEIR LOVE FOR US."

We went through a lot in these pages, and we finally made it to the conclusion. Hopefully, you haven't hurt any people because they weren't aligning with what you had planned for their dating life since you started this book.

So, what is the overall end to dating?

What is the end goal?

Marriage of course.

But that's another book for another time.

Finally, finding someone that you want to spend the rest of your life with, and knowing they have the same intentions for you is one of the greatest feelings I've known. It's near a sigh of relief when you know someone's digging you as much as you are to them; that nice feeling of knowing you have your own special person in your corner.

Now that you know where you're going after this crusade, there are two things I want to leave you with before we part ways.

The first is, there will never be anyone who checks all your dots all the time on your list. While I never want you to settle for someone or something that isn't a right fit for you, I would never want you to keep passing over good people because they don't meet every single requirement you would want. Now, all the basic requirements of being a partner, I would hope they would have them. But some of the more frivolous concerns of ours may never be met.

Understand that your partner is as worried, afraid, and anxious about this new stage in their life as well. You never know what will happen and what good would come about. So find yourself a good human, and don't chase someone who can't exist.

We're all human, we all disappoint and fail and we

do our best to make up for our shortcomings. Only you can decide on whether someone is worth taking the risk of dating. And only you should! You will have to live with the decisions of your life, not just the backseat drivers.

The last thing I want to mention before I head out: Never stop dating. I don't mean that in saying once you find someone good, go out and see if you can break your record for the best relationships in a month. What I mean is, never stop dating your partner. Never stop trying to learn more about them, trying to spend time with them, trying to love them and get them to smile.

The longer you're in a relationship, the easier it is to see that relationship as just another piece of your life. It's there. You know it's going to be there when you go to sleep because it was there when you woke up and it was there the week before. We get so comfortable and used to how life is that we forget to smell the flowers when we can.

And, while you are in a relationship, remember it is a relationship with a full, breathing person; someone who lets you know when you made their day and lets you know when they need to be held. You are with someone who has a heart as well, someone who likes to feel special just as much as you do. Never stop dating that person.

Life goes out before we have the time to jot down everything that happened. Always take the time to let your person know you see being with them as nothing short of an adventure, because, when we show how much we love others, they in turn show their love for us.

THINK ON THIS!

1. Finding someone that you want to spend the rest of your life with, and knowing they have the same intentions for you is one of the greatest feelings I've known.

2. Find yourself a good human, and don't chase someone who can't exist.

3. Only you can decide on whether someone is worth taking the risk of dating. And only you should!

4. The longer you're in a relationship, the easier it is to see that relationship as just another piece of your life.

5. Always take the time to let your person know you see being with them as nothing short of an adventure, because, when we show how much we love others, they in turn show their love for us.

A Brand NEW LIFE awaits you

If you have read this book and you want to willingly receive Jesus into your life as your personal Lord and Saviour, please bow your head and pray this prayer:

"My Heavenly Father, I come to You with all my heart. I repent of my sins and turn over completely to You. I confess that Jesus died for my sins and has become the Lord of my life from today. Write my name in the Lamb's Book of Life and blot it out of the Book of Death. I declare that I am washed clean from my sins by the Blood of Jesus. I am saved. Thank You Father, in Jesus' Name I pray. Amen!"

—Mike Dean: Grown & Alone…page 120

www.ingramcontent.com/pod-product-compliance
Lightning Source LLC
Chambersburg PA
CBHW020909080526
44589CB00011B/506